Gravity

Published by Creative Education
P.O. Box 227
Mankato, Minnesota 56002
Creative Education is an imprint of The Creative Company.

DESIGN AND PRODUCTION BY **ZENO DESIGN**

PHOTOGRAPHS BY Richard Cummins, Getty Images (Jim Bastardo,
Peter Cade, Lester Lefkowitz), Gayln C. Hammond, Tom Myers,
NASA, Tom Pantages (NASA), Photri-Microstock (Scott Berner),
Tom Stack & Associates (John Gerlach, NASA/JPL/TSADO, Greg
Vaughn), Unicorn Stock Photos (Jeff Greenberg, R. J. Mathews)

LIBRARY OF CONGRESS CATALOGING-IN-PUBLICATION DATA

Frisch-Schmoll, Joy.
Gravity / by Joy Frisch-Schmoll.
p. cm. — (Simple science)
Includes index.
ISBN 978-1-58341-576-4
1. Gravity—Juvenile literature. I. Title. II. Series.

QC178.F735 2008
530'.14—dc22   2007004184

First edition

9 8 7 6 5 4 3 2 1

SIMPLE SCIENCE

Gravity

Joy Frisch-Schmoll

CREATIVE EDUCATION

What goes up must come down. **Gravity**

(*GRAV-eh-tee*) makes this happen. If

you throw a ball into the air, it will fall

back down. A wagon will roll down a hill

because of gravity.

ROCKETS PUSH AGAINST GRAVITY

Gravity holds things in place. It stops things from floating away into outer space. Gravity pulls down on everything on Earth. It pulls people down. It pulls cars and houses down, too.

GRAVITY IS WEAK IN OUTER SPACE

Isaac Newton was a **scientist** (*SI-en-tist*) who lived a long time ago. He learned about gravity. He called things that push or pull "forces." Gravity is a force that pulls all things down to Earth.

Isaac Newton lived more than 300 years ago. He studied gravity after he saw an apple fall from a tree.

ISAAC NEWTON STUDIED GRAVITY

Gravity pulls on everything in the universe (*YOO-neh-vers*). The smallest piece of sand gets pulled by gravity. So do big things like the moon. Gravity keeps the moon close to Earth.

GRAVITY MAKES SAND FALL DOWN

Things that are big and heavy have lots of **mass**. The Earth has a lot of mass. The moon has less mass than Earth. The Earth and moon both have gravity. But Earth has stronger gravity because it has more mass.

PLANETS AND MOONS HAVE GRAVITY

GRAVITY

Things weigh less when gravity is weaker. The moon's gravity is not as strong as Earth's gravity. This means that **astronauts** (*AS-tro-nots*) weigh less on the moon than they do on Earth.

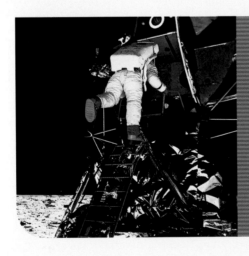

The moon's gravity is not very strong. If you were on the moon, you could jump a lot higher than you can on Earth.

PEOPLE FEEL LIGHT ON THE MOON

Gravity pulls hardest on heavy things. A big book will fall fast and make a loud crash if it is dropped. Snowflakes fall slowly. They make no sound when they land.

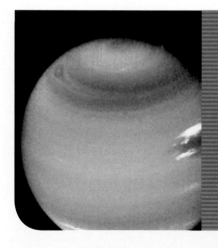

Gravity pulls Earth and the other planets into round shapes. That is why Earth is round, not square!

GRAVITY PULLS ON PEOPLE AND SNOW

When you jump rope, you are playing with gravity. Gravity pulls you back to the ground after each jump. When you play kickball, you are playing with gravity, too. Gravity pulls the ball down after you kick it.

IT CAN BE FUN TO JUMP AND LAND

Gravity is an important force. It keeps people and animals on the ground. It stops them from floating up into the air. Gravity holds the universe together!

Gravity makes roller coasters fun! It makes the cars go fast down the hills and loops.

GRAVITY PULLS DOWN ON WATER

22

You can see gravity in action. Get a book and a marble. Open the book and tilt it to make a ramp. Put the marble at the top of the ramp. Let go, and see what happens. Now put the marble at the bottom of the ramp. Try to roll it up with a gentle push. The marble is pulled by gravity. It rolls back down to the floor.

astronauts people who fly into outer space

gravity the force that pulls things down to Earth

mass how big or heavy something is

scientist a person who learns about science

universe everything on Earth and in outer space

23

24